HONEY POT PR

THE STORY OF RUFUS REDMAYNE

LOIS ELSDEN

Dedicated to the young people I have taught in Manchester, Oldham and Weston-super-Mare, especially students from SAIL PRU. You have been my inspiration!

Published by Honey Pot Press
2 The Dell, Worle
BS22 9LZ
www.honey-pot-press.co.uk
2013

ISBN 978-1-909627-01-7

Lois Elsden has taught in inner-city schools and pupil referral units for many years before giving up work to write full time. Her work for young people is aimed at reluctant readers, those who can read but are reluctant to do so.

Run, Blue, Run!

Screaming King Harry

She has also produced a guide to writing for young adults and anyone wishing to write creatively

The Story of Rufus Redmayne

Novels for adults:

Farholm

The Stalking of Rosa Czekov

Loving Judah

night vision

Flipside

www.loiselsden.com

THE STORY OF RUFUS REDMAYNE

1

Rufus Redmayne was a strange boy. He had few friends but those he had were good and loyal. He was always happy in his own company and never tried to make friends for the sake of it. He had a loving family and he was particularly close to his grandmother.

Rufus's grandmother was Ruby Redmayne and she too had a solitary nature and lived alone and happily in a cottage in the middle of Camel Wood.

It became routine for Rufus to visit Ruby on a Sunday morning. He was never one to lie in and sometimes, in the summer, in the hot days of July and August, he would be out on his bike and racing through Camel Wood as early as five while all the world seemed to be asleep.

In Camel Wood there are many eyes belonging to many creatures. However early Rufus rode among the trees, taking the woodland paths, there would be eyes upon him. He always saw the birds, busy finding food for young families, and often there were squirrels in the branches or on the ground. Occasionally a late fox slunk across his path, and a couple of times he glimpsed the shadowy form of a deer.

And there were times when Rufus felt other eyes upon him and wondered if there was a traveller or wildman hiding in the undergrowth. He never saw Wulf Lupus, standing as still as a stag in the shadow of a smooth-barked tree.

Rufus's mother, Maria, sometimes worried at the thought of her son alone in the wood and would telephone Ruby during the morning to check he had arrived safely.

"You will be careful, Rufus," Maria said

"Of course, mum," he replied.

"There are strange people out and about in the woods," she went on, trying not to sound too anxious.

"Well, I've never seen any," Rufus said.

"A lot of strange things have happened in Camel Wood," Maria went on.

"Such as? What strange things?"

"People going missing, children getting lost."

"Don't worry about me, Mum, I'll be fine."

WOMAN MISSING IN WOOD DRAMA

"Come home Gran," Rufus, 15, urges.

Concern was mounting yesterday for 62 year-old Ruby Redmayne of Todd Cottage, Camel Wood. The reclusive Mrs Redmayne was last seen on Tuesday by her daughter-in- law Maria when they met to go shopping at Camel Mall, just outside Castair.

"She was her usual self," said Maria, 42. "We had a good look round the shops, had lunch and then went our separate ways. I can't understand it. I'm very worried for her."

The alarm was raised by her football-mad 15 year-old grandson Rufus.

He cycled over to see Mrs Redmayne on Sunday morning to find her doors open and no sign of his grandmother.

"I always see Gran on Sundays, I don't know where she can be."

The police refuse to comment on local reports that large animal paw prints have been seen in and around the cottage.

"The Great Beast of Camel is just a local myth," said a police spokesman.

Anyone with information on the whereabouts of the missing 62 year-old woman should contact Strand Street Police Station in Castair on 012345678910

3

THE GREATY BEAST OF CAMEL

'Tis said that Camel Wood was once a mighty forest stretching from where the sea meets the shore a thousand leagues to where King Arthur held his court.

'Tis said that deep within old Camel Wood, mighty beasts roamed, bears, wolves and huge boars with tusks as sharp and as keen as the sharpest, keenest blade in all the land.

'Tis said that some of these strange beasts came from a time when magic was a power stronger than any man's prayer.

Now, 'tis said that even in these modern times, when Camel Wood is small and kept by man, that deep within the old wood at witching times, strange beasts have sway.

The witching times are those times, neither day nor night, neither night nor day. The witching times are the times of half-light, of dusk and dawn and dawn and dusk, and at these times, 'tis said that then strange beasts do roam.

Of all those strange beasts, the one man and woman do most fear is the Greaty Beast.

The Greaty Beast was born of times when pestilence was on the land. 'Twas a time when hunger, death and plague drove men and women and children to do ungodly things.

'Tis said the Greaty Beast is a creature of the witching hours, and even today, the Greaty Beast waits and watches for the unwary.

And in the towns of Camel Wood, those towns which once were hams and cots, those towns of Castair to the East and Strand to the West, Oak to the South and Easthope to the North, the most feared of the Greaty Beasts was given a name.

Part wolf, part man, part witch, part elf, Wulf Lupus watched for the unwary, from behind the trees.

4

SEND IN SNIPERS TERRIFIED TOWNSFOLK TELL TAYLOR

Residents of towns and villages near Camel Wood are demanding that something should be done to protect them from the beast which has slaughtered a number of sheep in the area.

"My texel ram weighed 11stone. It was torn apart. I found its remains all across the field," said farmer Mark Davis from Camel Farm, Camel Wood. "I am frightened that a child might be the next one to be found ripped to pieces."

"I have carcasses of two ewes with their throats torn out," said his neighbour Jane Smith. "The police should do something."

The police in Strand have confirmed that three different incidents of mutilated livestock have been received from farmers in the Bethel area. "Our investigation has revealed further sightings: three separate reports have come in from Little Oak, two from Oak and an incredible seven from Hope Village". Since our previous coverage of a similar incident where Bully, a Staffordshire bull terrier was killed in his Easthope garden, two other dogs and a cat have been found dead by their Easthope owners.

Chief Inspector Michael Taylor has been asked by a group of concerned residents to bring in a marksman to hunt and kill the animal.

"I have asked my officers to give me a full report," said Inspector Taylor. "We are fully committed to protecting the people and their pets and livestock."

Jeremy Harmer, an expert on big cats, has gathered evidence which he will give to Inspector Taylor tomorrow.

"I have casts of paw prints found in Camel Wood, Bethel and Hope Village. I have droppings found in Easthope which may be connected to the animal which slaughtered Bully. I will be giving it all to the police tomorrow," said Mr Harmer.

Unlike the beasts of Bodmin (Cornwall) Portballintrae (Northern Ireland) and Dumfries (Scotland) which have been identified as large cats, the Beast of Camel is said to resemble a large grey dog or wolf.

"Someone will get hurt unless the police do something now," said Mark Davis.

5.

I shouldn't have punched him on the nose, sir, I know I shouldn't but I wasn't thinking straight.

Sorry sir.

Yes, I know I should be saying sorry to him but he deserved it. He did deserve it; he shouldn't have said those things about my Nan. I don't care what he calls me, they can call me weird or a gimp or a creep or whatever but he shouldn't say those things about my Nan.

Yes, sir, you can bet I'm upset. How would you feel, sir if your grandma went missing?

He said she'd gone off with that bloke who lives in the forest.

Which bloke? I don't know his name, he works for the Forestry Administration.

Have I told the police?

Told the police what? About the bloke who lives in the forest? There's nothing I can tell them about him. But there are people who live in the forest. What people? I dunno, I dunno. No I don't know. It's just what people say. Stories, stories most like.

No I don't want to sit down, no I don't want a drink. I just want to go home to my mum. She'll be in a right state if I'm in trouble. It's bad enough with my Nan without you ringing her up.

Yes, I know it's my fault. Yes, I'll apologise. But I reckon he ought to apologise for calling my Nan.

Okay, yeah I will have a drink, yeah I do feel a bit faint. No, I didn't have any lunch, my mum forgot to make it and I forgot too. Breakfast? I didn't feel like any. There's a policewoman at the house and my aunty and neighbours and I just wanted to get away.

The stories about the people who live in the wood? I dunno. They're only stories, you know, tales, legends, yes, myths and legends – we did it in year 7. The teacher made an anthology, we all got a copy, Myths of Camel Wood. But the thing is, no-one knows Camel Wood, not like I do. No-one goes in it much, too spooky, creeps them out, they say.

I know Camel Wood. I know where the old quarry is and I know where the violets grow, and wild garlic, blackberries, hazels. I know where you can find truffles – yeah, truffles, fungi, my Nan showed me. She could make a fortune selling them but we prefer to keep it to ourselves, they're nice in scrambled eggs.

I know where the badger setts are, and the foxes' dens. I know Camel Wood and that there are things there. Things? Yeah, squirrels, deer and foxes. There are people who live there. Gypsies, well, yes there are gypsies and travellers. Some of them leave a right old mess... not the real gypsies, I know some of them and they've shown me things. How to set a snare, how to make pegs and baskets.

So what things do I mean? I dunno, sir, I dunno.... You'll think I'm stupid.

Well, ok. I reckon there are wolves in the wood. Not escaped ones I don't mean. I think in the old wood – Camel Wood is old sir, really old, part of it used to be the Great Wood, my Nan says. I think in the old wood there used to be wolves. There's a gravestone in Oak church for an old lady who was eaten by a wolf in 16 something. There's a notice that says the last wolf was killed in these parts just after that but I reckon there are still some in Camel Wood.

No, of course I don't think they attacked my Nan. If they had, the police would have found something.

Thanks for the drink sir, I do feel a bit... it's thinking about my Nan... wondering.

Other stories? Um, well... there's supposed to be wild men living in the wood. Not tramps, I don't mean, I mean sort of like wild men, like primitive... You know like the tribes in the Amazon, hidden tribes. They're supposed to be covered in hair and live in the woods. There are caves, near where the old quarry is. Its' just a story sir, though sometimes....

13

And then there's this sort of monster. That is just a story though sir. This monster is supposed to be like a wolf but like a human. Sort of werewolf sort of thing. But I think that's just the same story as the wild men except they're peaceful and timid, shy like deer, and he's fierce and dangerous.

But these are just stories.

Can I go now sir?

6

His heart was beating so loudly it seemed that all the wood was filled with the sound of it. His hot breath wheezed in and out, in and out, whistling and rasping. His whole body seemed turned to jelly, as if his bones had melted with terror.

Rufus lay in the ditch beneath the fallen tree, not daring to look, fearing not to in case someone, something came upon him as he lay cowering in the mud and rotting leaves.

What was it that he had seen? He tried to make sense of the images that flicked before his staring eyes, stinging with sweat, tears and blood.

And where was the girl?

Gradually his breathing quietened and he became aware of something sticking into his shoulder, a rock or a stone. There was a sharp twig jabbing into his leg. But he daren't move. Daren't make a sound.

He seemed to have lost his hearing as he had run for his life, tearing through the undergrowth, sprinting between the trees, falling, tumbling, scrambling to his feet and running, running...

He wondered if he was still deaf because he could hear nothing, but, moving his head slightly a leaf rustled against his ear. The wood was silent. Strangely, weirdly, un-naturally silent, as if before a storm when the wind drops.

Then a bird shrieked and all the other birds began to sing as they did at dawn when the light begins to return to the sky.

What had he seen? What was it...?

***

Sick of school, not wanting to go home to his mother, grieving and frightened as she waited for news of her mother, Rufus had gone into Camel Wood.

He had raced along the familiar paths, jumping his bike over banks and ditches. And every so often he had called his gran's name.

Then suddenly something was in front of him and he swerved and skidded and landed painfully up against a tree.

The girl looked at him and laughed.

"You stupid wazzock!", she said.

Rufus knew her, had seen her around school, had seen her often enough standing outside the head's room. She was always in trouble Naimh Locke she was called. Mostly because of her name. She got so mad if it was mispronounced but who on earth could tell it was pronounced "neeve" just from looking at it?

He had seen her in a fight in the dining hall. A lad had said something to her and she had jumped across a table and laid into him. It had been impressive. Perhaps Rufus wouldn't get so picked on if he fought like that...

And then he remembered the incident in the cloakroom when Horner had called his gran and Rufus had punched him straight on the nose. It had been spectacular, blood everywhere and Horner screaming like a pig. Well, he was a greedy pig. Rufus wouldn't get any trouble from him again.... But if he was permanently excluded he'd never see him again anyway.

"What you staring at then, Rooftop? You got a tile loose?" and Naimh laughed.

"I'm looking for my gran," he said.

"I'd like to find my gran too," Naimh said, almost friendly.

"Is she missing? Did she disappear?" Perhaps there was a pattern, perhaps it would give a clue to what had happened to Ruby if there were other people who had disappeared.

"No, it was my Mum what disappeared."

"Kidnapped?"

"No! God you are a gimp! No she dumped me when I was a little kid. I thought everyone knew that! I'm the

Tracey Beaker of the school – you can't tell me nothing about kids' homes and foster parents!"

"What about your dad?"

"What's a dad?" Naimh spoke with brittle bitterness. "Want a fag?"

"Go on then," Rufus didn't smoke but was so desperate for a friendly word that he was prepared to accept anything. Also, he was somewhat terrified of Naimh. She had masses of reddy gold hair stuck out in an Afro. There were random plaits with beads woven into them. She looked like a female pirate. She was very frightening with her Goth make-up. "I've been kicked out of school."

"Good for you. What for?"

"Horner was calling my gran so I decked him," it was a slight exaggeration but it sounded better than the truth. The truth was Rufus had lashed out at random and caught Horner full in the face with a wild blow.

"Fat get, serves him right. I got done for trashing Baird's house."

"*Mr Baird!?*"

"Yes, Mr Baird our beloved head teacher."

Rufus was impressed. He'd not met Mr Baird but had been taught cookery by his wife. She was called Edwina.

What sort of posy name was that? And she had favourites, called them her poppets. Rufus wasn't a poppet.

"What you laughing at?" Naimh demanded in a threatening way, ready to lash out.

"I bet you weren't one of Mrs B's poppets, were you?" said Rufus, unable to contain his laughter.

To his relief Naimh's fierce face relaxed and she laughed too.

"You're ok, Rooftop," she said. "Come on I know a place where we can sit down. Come on."

They began to walk through the wood, Rufus pushing his bike. At one point he tentatively asked if Naimh would call him 'Rufus' not 'Rooftop'. To his relief she punched his arm lightly and said 'right on, cool,' which was a reference to the way Mrs Baird tried to be what she called 'with it'.

For the first time in a very long time, Rufus had felt almost happy. Walking with someone, talking about stuff, making them laugh at things he said.

They were walking through the woods... just walking... the trees getting more dense.... The undergrowth higher and thicker... Just talking...

When suddenly there was this noise. A howl, a shriek, a bloodcurdling growling, throat-stopping, heart-

19

wrenching... and before them.... A thing... jaws.... Teeth.... Slavering... crouched ready to leap... its eyes.... Its eyes...

And they had run, run for their lives.

7

Scene: the casualty department in Strand Royal Hospital. It is a typical early evening, a few people waiting, some with obvious injuries, some just sitting, grey-faced and anxious.

Enter a man in jeans and a camouflage jacket. He's helping a boy who looks in a state of shock and can hardly walk; his legs would buckle except the man is holding him up. There is a trickle of blood down the side of his face and his clothes are rumpled and muddy, he only has one shoe.

Receptionist:	Yes?
Man:	Hello. I've got this young lad here, I found him collapsed in Camel Wood. He's hit his head and I can't get much sense out of him. I think he may be concussed.
Receptionist:	Name?
Man:	Jack Green.
Receptionist:	Age?
Man	38

Receptionist: Not your age, his age?

Man: Sorry. I don't know. (to the boy) Hey, lad, how old are you?

Boy: (*mumbles*)   15

Man: He's 15.

Receptionist: (*sarcastically*) Yes, I got that thank you. Jack Green, age 15.

Man: He's not Jack Green, I am – I don't know who he is, I just found him. What's your name, lad?

Boy: Rufus, I'm Rufus Redmayne. Where's the girl, where's Naimh?

Jack :   I didn't see any girl.

Receptionist: (*being helpful at last*) Where do you live, Rufus?

Rufus: Where's Naimh? There was this wolf thing – big, big as you, sir.

Jack to receptionist: He's been going on about being attacked by a wolf. I think he's hallucinating. (*To Rufus*) Where do you live, lad? What's your address?

Rufus: Little Hope.

Receptionist: Little hope of what?

Jack :   It's a village near Camel Wood, Little Hope.

Receptionist (*annoyed*) Well, I didn't know. I've only just moved here.

Rufus: 5, The Cottages, Plough Lane.

Receptionist: Next of kin?

Rufus: My mum, Maria, Maria Redmayne. I'm not hallucinating. There really was a – a thing – you know the Greaty Beast? I saw it!

Receptionist: (*to Jack*) What's he on about?

Jack :   It's a local tale, it's been in the news because of these farmers that have had their stock attacked.

Rufus: (*trying to get himself together*) I'm not making it up. I was walking with this girl and suddenly…. We saw it, it was massive… we ran, ran… Where's Naimh, where's Naimh?

Receptionist: Try to stay calm, young man. Date of birth?

Rufus: (*drags at Jack's arm, tries to pull him*) We've got to find Naimh, she's in the wood!

Jack :   Calm down, lad, calm down. I didn't see anyone, you were just lying there in the mud. I bent over to get you up, you screamed and passed out. There was no girl there.

Rufus: We must find her! She's in danger!

Rufus pulls away from Jack , turns and stumbles towards the exit, limping and staggering as if he might fall at any moment. Jack catches him up, stops him but is looking at Rufus's jacket.

24

Jack :   What's happened to your
                    jacket, it's all ripped?

Rufus   We've go to find Naimh!

Jack : (*almost shouting*) What happened to your
                    jacket?

*Jack pulls Rufus jacket off and holds it up,
examining it. There are great rips and tears.*

Jack : (*speaking calmly now*) Did this beast thing
                    chase you?

Rufus: (*also calm as he realises that Jack is
listening to him now*) I think so. I just ran, I could
                    hear it panting in my ear, I
                    thought I could feel its breath
                    on my neck but I think I was
                    just imagining that. It grabbed
                    my jacket, tried to pull me
                    back. It's a good thing it's just
                    a cheapo charity shop one, it
                    just ripped and I got away.

Jack :   What did it grab you with?

Rufus: (*he looks shocked by the question as if he
suddenly realises what has*

happened to him) Oh my God.
Oh my God. (*his legs give way
and he sinks to the floor*)

Jack : (*speaking coldly and calmly*) Tell me what
happened?

Rufus: It got my jacket with its
mouth, its teeth... its teeth... It
was a wolf thing.... But it was
running after me... running
after me on two legs.

8

DW: Good evening and this is Dinah Weston bringing you this evening's news on Coast TV. And our breaking news is that there has been another disappearance from Camel Wood. Police are still investigating the mystery of the whereabouts of 62 year-old grandma, Ruby Redmayne. They are now searching the wood and surrounding areas for 15-year-old schoolgirl, Naimh Locke.

Coast TV special correspondent, Kenny Kenton, now brings you this report. Kenny.

KK: Dinah. Yes and as you can probably see behind me police are mounting a massive search for 15 year-old Naimh who hasn't been seen since lunchtime today. It is unusual for this sort of response from the police so soon after someone is reported missing, but this comes in the light of the continuing mystery of the whereabouts of Ruby Redmayne, missing from her cottage in Camel Wood for over a week now. Dinah.

DW: Kenny, yes and I believe the police are investigating a connection between Ruby's grandson and Naimh.

KK: You're right, Dinah. Rufus Redmayne, a schoolmate of Naimh's was the last person to have seen her. He is at present in Strand Royal Hospital. He was found unconscious in the wood by Forest Agent Jack Green. As you probably remember, Dinah, Rufus reported his grandma missing. He claims he went to visit her and she was not in her cottage.

DW: What do we know about Rufus, Kenny?

KK: Not much Dinah. Apparently he and Naimh were both suspended from school for unrelated incidents.

DW: Thank you Kenny. This is Coast TV bringing you the latest news from around the region. And following Kenny Kenton's report on missing schoolgirl Naimh Locke, we go to our education correspondent Tracey Winters who is at St Finbarr's High, the school where both these young people were students. Tracey.

TW: Dinah. Yes and I am here outside St Finbarr's High where in the past few minutes headmaster Edward Baird has made the following statement.

(Cut to Mr Baird)

Mr Baird: First of all I would like to extend our sympathy to the parents of Naimh and the mother of Rufus at this difficult time. We will do all we can to aid the police in finding Naimh and we hope and pray she will be returned safe and unharmed to her family.

TW: Mr Baird, Tracey Winters, Coast TV. Mr Baird, is it true both students were suspended from school.

Mr Baird: Indeed. Following a serious incident in school today Rufus was sent home after we had contacted his mother. This is not a permanent exclusion. Naimh has not been in school for three days on a fixed term exclusion.

TW: Is it true, Mr Baird, that Naimh was suspended for vandalising your house?

Mr Baird: I cannot comment.

TW: Mr Baird can you comment on the fact that your son, Ed, had been bullying Naimh and she broke into your house with the intention of reclaiming some property she claims he had taken from her?

Mr Baird: No comment.

TW: Reports in the press have suggested that she trashed your kitchen, broke furniture in Ed's room.

Mr Baird: No comment. Thank you ladies and gentlemen.

(Cut back to Tracey)

TW: After that brief statement Mr Baird went back into the school. We are expecting a further update from the police. This is Tracey Winters, Coast TV, returning you to the studio.

(Cut back to Dinah)

DW: Police spokesmen have refused to comment on the report of armed response officers on the scene. This is linked to the supposed sighting of a large wolf-like creature, and the attacks on farm stock in the area.

And now, before the rest of today's news from Coast TV we go to our weather-room where Stewart has an important severe weather warning for us. Stewart.

(Cut to Stewart in the weather room)

Stewart: Thank you, Dinah. Good evening and sorry folks, if you aren't already experiencing torrential rain, high winds and a dramatic drop in temperature, you soon will. The police searching the Camel Wood area will be the first to bear the brunt of this mini weather system coming in from the east...

9

Jack stopped a couple of hundred yards short of the police barrier. There was a crowd of reporters and a couple of TV vans, their antennae beaming the latest details back to their studios. With a grim smile he reversed his jeep than turned and drove back down the Strand Road. A mile further on he turned down a track, stopped, unlocked the gate across it and drove through. He was about to lock it behind him but then thought a quick escape might be needed.

He did not know what lay ahead, he did not know what was lurking deep within Camel Wood but the rips on the back of the boy's coat had alarmed him.

There had been spots of rain on his windscreen as he had sped along Strand Road, now his wipers were full on clearing the water from the glass. Above him the tall conifers were waving backwards and forwards as if trying to flag him down to stop. The sky had become a curious greeny yellow colour and the light had a dense, opaque quality. This was not the weather for anyone to be out in the wood.

He pulled over and jumped out. He took his waterproofs from the boot and unlocked and opened his gun case. He loaded the shotgun he took from it and slipped a handful of spare cartridges into each pocket. He wasn't worried by the moaning sounds from among the trees, they were the normal noises of a forest in the wind but there was a curious low humming groan like a beast in pain.

He wondered about a girl out there alone... wondered if she was still alive.

He had no doubt that Ruby was dead. He knew her slightly, had met her early mornings out in the wood. She was tall and unsmiling but had been friendly enough. More than once she had given him a bag of fungi she had collected, he'd had a good breakfast thanks to Ruby Redmayne.

He stopped, his hands tightening on his gun; there was a distant howl, as spine chilling as a lone wolf baying at the moon. But there were no wolves in Camel Wood, it must be a police dog.

There was a shrieking noise now adding to the tumult of the storm. Jack had been in the woods in all seasons and in all weathers but never had he heard such sounds. The hairs on the back of his neck rose as he felt someone watching him through the driving rain. He spun round, cocking his gun, his finger on the trigger and almost shot Rufus.

"Bloody hell, lad!" he yelled. "I bloody nearly shot you! What the hell are you doing here! Trying to get yourself killed?"

"We need to find Naimh!" the boy said. He was wearing a hooded raincoat which Jack recognized as his own. It had been tossed in the back of the jeep. That's where Rufus had hidden himself.

"No *we* don't, *I* do. You get back in the jeep, you lock the doors and the windows, you keep your head down and you stay there until I get back."

"No!"

"Do as I say."

"Or? Look, mister, either you take me with you so you know where I am or you set off and I follow you."

Jack stared through the sheeting rain at the boy who stood before him.

"OK, lad, but you do exactly as I say, I don't want to blow your head off by mistake."

"I've been thinking. I think I know where they are. Come on I'll show you."

Jack grabbed Rufus's arm.

"You know where they are?"

"In the Old Fort" Rufus turned abruptly and began to trot into the forest.

Astounded, Jack was slow to follow and then had to run to catch him.

"The Old Fort doesn't exist, it's just a fairy tale!" he grabbed at the boy's arm but his hands slipped on the wet sleeve and Rufus dashed away from him.

Jack ran too. And as he ran he kept glancing back, trying to see through the lashing branches and the tossed leaves, trying to make out through the streaming rain exactly what seemed to be following them.

10

I ran down the trackway, so small it had to be a badger's, ducking beneath the hanging branches, pushing through the dead briars not caring that they whipped across my face. I jumped over fallen boughs, not running away from the thing now but running to its lair. My heart was pounding, the breath rasping in and out of my chest. I had ached all over from running away from the thing, the beast before but now my legs were strong. I had to find Gran, I had to find the girl before it was too late.

How could I not have realised where Gran was, where the girl was too? How could I have been so stupid? I'd even told Mr Smith about the wild men and the monster, I'd told him about the caves near the quarry.

Of course, they were in the Old Fort. The forester, Jack, had said it was a fairy tale. Well so is the Greaty Beast, so are the Wild Men.

Jack was behind me, shouting for me to stop and wait, but there wasn't any time.

It was raining even harder and it was getting darker, partly because the light was going out of the sky, partly because deep in the deepest part of the wood, as you climb up towards the old quarry the woods get very dark.

There isn't a proper way to the caves, you just sort of come across it even if you know the wood really well like I do. It is supposed to be hidden by some sort of spell, but that's just rubbish really. It's just old tales.

I stopped running. I stood really still. Animals have another sense; they can sense danger even before they can smell it. That was me at that moment. There was danger all around, crackling like static.

Jack crashed into me and we both fell over and tumbled down a slope into a little gully.

"Be quiet now," I hissed. "Quiet."

He stared at me as we crouched in the gully. The rain was pattering on the leaves above us, trickles of water ran somewhere.

"Listen," I whispered.

He could hear it too. Something was out there, snuffling for our scent.

Jack cocked his gun and the click echoed.

"Where are we?"

"We're nearly there," I couldn't tell him that the path would find us not the other way round.

I couldn't tell him either that his bullet would have no power against the monster. We were safe where we were, the ramsons all around us. Ramsons smell; some people think they stink, other people know they are wild garlic. I pulled up clumps of the stuff now and stuffed it down my shirt and into my pockets.

"What the hell are you doing?" Jack looked at me as if I was mad, his moustache bristling.

"Garlic – my Gran says it protects you."

He looked at me as if I was even madder.

"We're safe down here, it won't come down here, it doesn't like garlic," I told him and handed him a bunch of the broad-leafed plant.

There was a sort of snarling above us and we cowered against the mossy bank. The noise moved away.

"You mean it's like... like a .... But they don't exist, vampires, that sort of thing..." his face was white. He was a man who didn't scare easily, I guessed. He was scared now.

"Like a were-wolf," I whispered and my heart gave a sort of jolt.

He took the garlic and did as I did, stuffing bunches of it into his jacket.

I took a handful and bent it over, snapping the stems then rubbed the juice over my face and stamped on it getting its stink all over the bottoms of my shoes.

"Your wife's going to love you," I said as he did the same. I don't know why I was joking, it wasn't funny.

"Now what?" he grunted.

"We have to find the secret path, come on."

11

. . . Camel was once rich in minerals including lead, silver, zinc, tin, copper and lupusite[1] and there are many disused mines and shafts in the area. Lead, silver and lupusite were the main ores mined. There was, in earlier times, some zinc, tin and copper mining, but the deposits of these metals were poor, and not worth excavating. Some of these mines date back to Roman times although most of the older ones have long since collapsed, or fallen in, or been filled by spoil from other workings.

There was industrial-scale quarrying and open cast mining as well as pits in the area, the remains of which can soon be detected once you have learned to read the landscape.

A warning! Although most shafts are capped there are many undiscovered in the area and when walking or exploring, one must always be aware that there could be deep and very dangerous shafts, uncapped and unmarked. Some of these shafts are

---

[1] Lupusite: extremely rare grey mineral, a metal only found in this area; said to deter evil spirits esp. werewolves, symbol Lp

many hundreds of feet deep. The deepest recorded one (now capped) is Old John (see map) This was named after John Copthorne who died after falling into the disused mine-shaft; he had worked there as a boy, and in his old age returned and fell to his death. His ghost is said to cry for help from the bottom of the shaft.

Still visible are the remains of adits[2] if you know where to look, or what to recognize. You may see hollows and depressions, which indicate where the mine-shaft may have run-in or collapsed, or bumps and uneven ground which may hint at fallen walls from buildings at the workings.

Ponds and spoil heaps[3] are another good indication that mining was once the main source of local employment. Water was necessary in many industrial processes including washing the galena[4]

Names of geographical features are also a good clue to the historical detective in reading the evidence of

---

[2] adit: opening or passage, esp. into a mine
[3] spoil heaps: waste from mining activities
[4] galena: lead ore, symbol LpS

42

the past. Horsetrough (see map), for example, is not named after a watering hole for horses but after the gin circle which was an important feature of shaft mining. It was a horse driven winding mechanism vital in the days before steam power.

Although there are traces of dangerous metals such as antimony[5], cadmium[6] and arsenic, their presence is at such a low level that for the casual rambler there is no danger. However it is not advisable to fill flasks or drink water from streams in the area.

There are, of course, a variety of different legends attached to Camel Wood, many much older and with less likelihood of being true than the sorry tale of Old John. There are many tales of hidden treasure; unlike the leprechauns[7] and their gold the local Camel trinxies[8] are said to guard crocks of silver. Romans are supposed to have buried a trove of denarii[9] hidden as the barbarians overran

---

[5] antimony: brittle bluish-white element, symbol Sb
[6] cadmium: a white metal, symbol Cd
[7] leprechaun: Irish pixie
[8] Trinxies: local name for pixie-like beings who dwell only in Camel Wood
[9] denary: silver money used by Romans

Britain, or maybe it was early Christian monks hiding the silver church plate in the face of the Viking onslaught (823AD Ingar Silverskin[10]) or even the Vikings themselves storing their booty. A mythical warrior, possibly Ingar, or perhaps St Finbarr[11] is supposed to sleep with his silver sword awaiting a call to defend the weak. This however, may merely be a local version of the Arthurian legend.

To start your walk, park your car at the Forestry Administration park by Fimbrook. . .

---

[10] Ingar Silverskin: Viking warrior who raided along the coast from Castair to Westope, raising the small port or Easthope (Estop) to the ground in 823AD)
[11] St Finbarr: son of Irish silver smith, patron saint of Cork, said to have visited Strand and Easthope in AD 601, reputed to have expelled a sea monster from a lake near Killarney and a similar beast from Camel Wood

12

We crept along the bottom of the gully. A stream had formed from the run-off down the sides and we splashed our way downwards. My feet were sodden and cold, I guess Jack had big waterproof boots on: he was that kind of man. We were sheltered from the worst of the weather raging above us. There were noises like I'd never heard before, and I've been in the woods in all weathers.

It was dark now, but as we came out into a wider gorge, there was a huge crack of thunder and lightning went across the sky in a great sheet. I could see the crags of the rocky outcrop up on our right, and in that flash they looked like the towers of a castle. It wasn't a castle, but back in the old times that was where the Old Fort was. I'd never seen it before, its one of those places that is sometimes there but sometimes not. But wherever it was, that was where Gran and Naimh were.

My legs were killing me, my feet were soaking, I hurt all over, but I ran up the slope towards Old Fort.

Jack was behind me, I could hear him panting. I glanced back.

"Look out!" I screamed.

I snatched up a rock and threw it, bowled it straight at the thing behind him.

Jack spun round just as my stone caught the thing right in the eye. It screamed, a noise enough to freeze a creature's blood. It couldn't be killed by such things but it could be hurt and I'd hurt it. Jack fired his gun and the creature stumbled over backwards and rolled down the incline.

"My God! What is it?" Jack shouted above the noise of the storm.

The rain was sheeting down almost like a curtain and in the dark the only way I knew to go was up.

"Come on," I shouted back "before it comes again."

"I killed it," Jack yelled back.

"Come on!" and I turned and ran. I couldn't explain that his bullet wouldn't kill that thing.

There was a sheer rock face ahead. Which way? I couldn't climb in this weather. I went right up to it. The rocks were covered in a sort of slimy moss and I couldn't have got up there even in the dry. I stood with my hands on the stone and I suddenly felt powerless.

"Come on, lad, let's go back," Jack came up beside me and leaning against the cliff.

"We have to find them," I said.

"I don't know what that thing was I killed but whatever it was that was what did for your Gran and that poor girl."

"Come on, this way," I said and set off along a track .

"We'd do better to go back into the wood, there's old mine workings up here. Dangerous shafts. We could fall to our deaths!" Jack grabbed my arm but I shook him off.

Jack muttered some swear words but he followed me all the same. We were following the face of the cliff and soon there were boulders and loose stones that rolled and slipped beneath our feet.

There was a way in, I knew there was, I just had to find it.

In the end it found me. I went past it, trod on a stone that moved beneath my foot so I stumbled and fell and my head and shoulders went into an empty space.

I could smell the stink of the creature. This was its lair.

13

"Come back, lad!" Jack shouted but he was standing alone in the teeming rain. The boy, Rufus had wriggled away from him into the jaws of the old mine.

There was a blinding streak of sheet lightning and then utter darkness. Cursing again, Jack bent and peered into the hole. He had fumbled a torch from his pocket and the beam played round the cave. The smell was almost overpowering; this had to be the den of whatever the thing was he had killed. Perhaps the boy was right and perhaps this would be where they would find what was left of the old woman and the girl.

Shuddering at the thought of bones and viscera Jack slid into the cave.

Bent almost double he followed the wet footprints left by Rufus, calling his name. He stopped as the tunnel forked into three. How would they get out? Their muddy footprints were clear enough on the bare rock at the moment but if they dried... Jack felt through his many pockets and came across a skein of twine he used in his duties around the forest. There was a pile of boulders to the left and he lashed the end of the twine around the largest and then played it out as he went deeper into the cave.

Unbidden thoughts of labyrinths containing monsters came into his mind, thoughts of a hero unwinding a thread to lead him back to daylight after he had slain the beast in the centre of the maze.

He called Rufus's name but there was no answering call.

He stooped lower then dropped to hands and knees to pass through a small passage.

"Rufus!"

"Here, Jack!" a distant voice ahead of him. He was on a slope, slippery with debris, small stones and rocks which rolled beneath his feet. The torch beam wavered and seemed to shrink but it was because he had entered a cavern with a pool. The water was still and black and the light did not reflect from it nor penetrate into it.

"Rufus! I'm by the pool!"

"This way!"

How did the boy know where to go? The voice had echoed from his right and there was a cleft in the rock face which Jack squeezed through. There was a rattle of stones from the slope he had just come down. Was Rufus behind him, had the acoustics deceived him? Jack pushed his way back through the cleft and shone his light round the cavern. No sign of the boy. The surface of the pool was rippling, moving as if disturbed by something.

A loose rock had fallen into it maybe... Spooked all the same Jack pushed back through the crack.

"I've found them! Jack! I've found them!!"

There was a sheer rock face ahead and no sign of any way forward.

"I've come to a dead end!" Jack shouted.

"You have to climb!"

Jack looked up and could see in the light of his torch there was a narrow opening at the top of the rock wall where it met the roof of the cave.

"Bloody hell," he muttered. He stripped off his waterproof, grasped his torch between his teeth and climbed the twelve-foot face. He misjudged the last pull and hit his head on an outcrop and the torch flew from his mouth and rolled away across the stony floor.

To his amazement he was not plunged into darkness, a faint glow came from the end of the narrow tunnel before him.

He heard a sound which almost froze his blood. A low, slavering snarl, a gurgling, guttural growl.

He glanced over his shoulder. Thrown into strange relief by the position of his torch on the floor, was a figure, crouching beneath him. Its shadow played upon the walls and it looked like a huge dog or wolf and yet, even as he stared down in horror at its gaping maw, it stood on its hind legs like a man and began to climb.

Jack lashed out with his foot and the creature recoiled before his boot even connected. The garlic smell of the ransoms? Panicking with terror Jack scrambled up into the tunnel and shuffled through towards the strange glow.

Before him was another cavern, low roofed and another pool but this cave was lit with a shimmering luminescence from the surface of the water.

"Jack! Jack!"

On the far side, on a hummock of glistening pebbles Rufus was with two other people.

Jack jumped down into the cave and ran across to them.

"You've got to help her!" Rufus cried.

The older woman was kneeling beside the girl patting her face. Both were soaking wet, the girl unconscious.

"She tried to swim out, she was convinced there was a way through the pool," the woman said, her teeth chattering with cold. "When she didn't come back I went in after her. Oh gods save her. I think I'm too late, I think she's drowned!"

"When did this happen?" Jack took the girl and laid her flat on the ground and tipped her head back. Her golden hair spread out like a mermaid's across the shiny stones. He opened her mouth to check her airways before he tried to revive her.

"Gran was just coming out of the pool with her when I came through!" Rufus exclaimed. He sounded near to tears.

"You know how to resuscitate? Come on let's go!"

Jack pinched the girls nose and blew into her mouth

The cavern echoed with a blood-chilling howl.

"Rufus! You carry on with the girl!"

Jack jumped to his feet. On the ledge above, the wolf thing crouched staring down at them. In the dim light of the phosphorescence the splash of blood and torn flesh on its chest was clearly visible.

"I – I thought I'd killed it!" Jack gasped.

"Here," the woman thrust something into his hand. To his amazement he realised it was a sword, a huge heavy silver sword.

"I'm not strong enough," she said. "You have to kill it. We're only safe here on the wolfblight." "Wolfblight?" Jack waved the sword about. It was heavy and unwieldy and his wet hand slipped on the hilt.

"These stones. Wolfblight... lupusite that's the scientific name. It won't come near us while we stay here." The woman had a deep gruff voice younger than her years.

There was the sound of coughing and the girl rolled away from Rufus and was sick, spluttering and retching.

"Look out!"

The thing had rushed at him while he was distracted by the girl.

Jack swung the sword but his feet slipped and he fell backwards and the creature was on him, its gaping jaws inches from his face. He smashed the pommel of the sword on its nose and it shook its head and he was able to slide away, roll over and get to his feet.

He took the sword in both hands and swung it in a huge arc and the creature leapt away out of his range.

It was massive. Standing on its back legs it was taller than Jack and he was over six foot. Unless he killed it they would be trapped here.

He wiped his hands on his trousers, grasped the sword more firmly and advanced on the beast. It dropped to its haunches as if cowed and Jack raised the sword. Lifting his arms had exposed his body and the monster leapt straight at his belly, its drooling jaws wide, lined with razor sharp teeth. Jack leapt to one side and the fangs sliced through his shirt. He swung the sword and caught it across its front paw.

It screamed and screeched, howled with pain and fury and twisted to attack again. The weight of the sword had pulled Jack round as he had swung it and he caught the full weight of the beast on his shoulder, its bony snout connecting with his head, its jaws snapping on the air, millimetres from his face.

Something hit Jack on the ear and something else and the beast jumped away. Rufus was throwing handfuls of lupusite pebbles.

It gave Jack the few seconds he needed to take his stand with the sword again. And this time he waited, standing as if playing cricket, the sword like a bat, poised to take the ball.

The monster sprung at him and this time Jack was ready, measuring his moment and, as its pounce was at its height, as it was about to drop on him, he swung two handed keeping his wrist straight and he caught the creature a sickening blow under its rib cage and he lifted it by its own momentum so it rolled over his head and tumbled screaming into the pool.

The luminous pool clouded and the water boiled and hissed and billows of steam erupted from the churning surface.

The creature's head emerged and it gave one last sickening roar of agony and rage then slid beneath the surface and was gone.

14

Ruby's diary

The old gods of the forest be thanked that I am returned to the upper world and am safe. Thanks too that the young girl, Naimh she be called, thank gods that she too be safe and unharmed.

I can't rightly say all that did happen to me, only that it were my own fault. I should have seen the signs, should have read them to know that Wulf Lupus had returned to Camel Wood and was seeking prey.

I know one day last week, I'm proper muddled now as to what day it be today, I were out gathering toadstools and mushrooms when he caught me. He threw something over me and carried me to his den. He were so strong he carried me as if I were a feather and gods know I'm a good body of a woman and no fairyweight.

✷✷✷

I lost my senses for a while as he ran through the forest but came to myself as he shoved me into his den up near the Old Fort.

I know all these old workings from when I were nowt but a spring chick and my granda used to take me exploring where his granda had taken him before. His granda were one of the last old miners and quarrymen and he worked with the sons of Old John Copthorne.

I hadn't been in these places for nigh on sixty years and as that Wulf Lupus threw me down I had no notion of where I might be save that it was fearful dark.

Now smoking is a filthy habit and tis something my dear Maria is forever telling me to give up but thank the old gods that I have never had the strength to do so because in that moment when that beast opened its foul jaws to gobble me up I sparked my lighter and he jumped away from the flame.

He could easily have knocked it from my hand but something took his fancy, maybe he heard something outside, maybe in the light he saw I was a shrivelled old thing but he turned and left me.

I could hear him outside howling and I was mortal afeared.

I took myself up and ran into the cave down the tunnel, thinking maybe I would find another way out. The old workings they be like a rabbit warren, a hundred different ways in, and a hundred different ways out.

And then I came to this wall and knew I would have to go back to find another way.

In my despair I cast my gaze upwards into the darkness but it wasn't dark and I knew I could find safety.

Now some old women eschew trousers. They keep my legs warm and dry when I'm out and about. They save me from scratches and prickles when I'm in the woods. So I went back to my childhood and climbed like a young girl unencumbered by skirts or petticoats or such.

I entered the shining cave and I knew where I be. Granda had brought me here. This be the last place where there is wolfblight. I read books, I read books about old Camel and I know that this be properly called lupusite. But I know from granda that lupusite be mortal to Wulf Lupus and his kind. The shining pool glows with lupusite traces, harmless to man but lethal to the kin of Wulf Lupus.

I know not how many days and nights I sat by the pool. I searched the cave but there was no other way out. The way granda had brought me those many years ago must have fallen in.

The beast would stick his foul head though the tunnel and bay at me, but I put my hood over my head and stayed sat prettily on the wolfblight.

I did find some silver and some gold. So the stories of old treasure were true. And one thing I did find were a mighty silver sword as big as me. Silver will kill those things which cannot be slain by other metals but I were not strong enough to lift it. So I sat and I waited...

And then the girl came...

15

Rufus's diary

Dere diry, well im ok and I found gran and naimb and jack was with me. I was ded scard cos the wulf thingy the weerwulf nerly got us but jakc had this sord wot gran found. It was made of silver and silver is dedly to weerwolfs

Jack fell over and I thort the wulf wuld kill him but he sumhow got it off him. he ataked it with the sord and cut the wulf and then the wulf nearly got him.

I chukd the wulfblite at it and it bakd off and jack got up and the wulf ran at him and jack swung the sord and I dunno how he did it but he sort of liftd the wulf onhis sord into the pool. Wel that was the end it was orful the water boyled an this smoke came off and the wulf screemed and then went under the water and that was the end.

Jack and me had to give naimb the kiss of life and she wos ok I never thort id need that wen we did it in first aid at scool but there you go. gran was ok I was so pleesd to see her I new she wasnt ded but I just didnt no wen I wuld see her and here she was alrite.

We had to get out of the cave gran was realy week cos she hadnt eaten for days just drunk the water from the shinning pool I wuldnt fancy that. now naimb was ok but she sed she felt wobbly so jack and me helped them. It was difficult getting down the wall I stayd at the top and jack went down first then naimb then gran then me we was all shaking and ded cold and we all felt like crying but we were so nerly safe.

Jacks torch was still there and his green string so we got out of the cave and the rain had stopped and ther was a full moon and jack sed wed better watch out for werewolves but it wasnt funny

 Nan and naimbh had to go to hopsicle I just went home to mum with jakc.

So that is the end of the graty beest .

 thank god were ok or as gran wld say thank the old gods of camel wood

16

Naimh's journal

Dear Naimh, I cannot believe I am safe, I really thought I was going 2 get raped and tortured and killed. I feel sick now just thinking about it, I could puke right now just thinking about it. I met that gimp Rufus except I shouldn't call him that now since he saved my life and that guy Jack.

Anyway I was with Rufus when and this is what I can't really believe even tho it happened 2 me it seems like a dream.

Anyway there was this thing. I think it was some deformed man or maybe it was a wolf that had been cloned or an experiment of genetic engineering. There's a research station near Castair perhaps they did an experiment what went wrong.

This sounds mad but it is true.

Anyway this wolf or werewolf or whatever carried me 2 its den I screamed and screamed and suddenly out of the dark this mad old woman ran and threw a big shiny stone @ it and it let go. The old woman grabbed me and we ran back in2 the tunnel I don't know how she could see in the dark but she just led me till we could go no further and then she made me climb this wall.

I h8 PE and this sort of thing but with that werewolf behind me I went up that wall as quick as anything and the old woman 2.

We came into this big cave with a shining pool and she made me sit on these shiny stones, wolfblight she called them she said we'd b safe.

She was Rufus's nan, the old lady who disappeared. She sort of collapsed on the stones, she was really weak cos she hadn't eaten anything 4 all the days she had been missing.

I had 2 escape I couldn't bear 2 b trapped in the cave I kept thinking of all the rocks and earth above us and imagining them coming crashing down.

Ruby tried 2 calm me down but the time just went on and on and I knew we would just die here.

Ruby had found a big silver sword but she could hardly lift it and nor could I.

She said we had 2 just w8 , help would come. I got proper noughty with her and we had a row but then I calmed down and said sorry and I started crying. I h8 it when I cry.

God we sat there hours. I kept thinking that Rufus was dead because otherwise he would have got someone 2 rescue us. I didn't say this 2 his nan.

I kept getting panic attacks, I tried 2 keep calm and b strong but I have claustrophobia and it was really bad in the cave and the shining water was really creeping me out. I kept staring @ it and I thought I could see like a light. I thought this must b a tunnel 2 outside. I thought it must b day outside and the light shining through.

Ruby and I had a massive row because I wanted 2 try 2 swim out. I'm a good swimmer. I h8 sport but swimming is ok.

In the end I won the argument cos I just pulled off my trainers and coat and jumped in. . .

Big mistake. I nearly drowned.

I had dived under the water and started swimming but then I realised I was nearly out of breath. I turned 2 go back but my lungs were bursting and suddenly I had 2 open my mouth and all the water came in and there were all these bubbles all round my head and the next thing I remember was being sick in the cave.

Being sick in front of Rufus, How shaming is that!

And there was this guy with a sword fighting the wolf.

My god this sounds mad.

Perhaps I hallucinated the whole thing. Except 4 the teeth marks in my jacket

The Story of Rufus Redmayne is written as a guide to story-telling using different ways of progressing the narrative; this is ideal for students who may be asked to write in a variety of ways for examination purposes. Each chapter offers an example of how a story may be written, but 'Rufus' can also be used to encourage reluctant readers, those able to read and read fluently, but who are reluctant to do so.

The Story of Rufus Redmayne

Contents: Page

Also by Lois Elsden:

Run, Blue, Run!
Who are the three men in black, and why are they after Blue? Followed by these sinister men, Blue can only do one thing... *run!*

Screaming King Harry

Who shot popular teacher Henry King? Who is threatening Jo-Jo and her family? Her friend Tofuzul is on the run, and Jo-Jo runs with him, she has to find the truth and save herself and those she loves!